The Boyer Lectures

Each year the ABC invites a prominent Australian to present the results of his or her work and thinking on major social, scientific or cultural issues in a series of radio talks known as the Boyer lectures.

The series was inaugurated in 1959 under the title of the ABC lectures, but in 1961 the ABC re-named the series as a memorial to the late Sir Richard Boyer. As chairman of the ABC, Sir Richard had been one of those chiefly responsible for the introduction of the original series.

1987 Boyer Lectures

Piecing Together a Shared Vision

Davis McCaughey

Published by ABC Enterprises for the
AUSTRALIAN BROADCASTING CORPORATION
20 Atchison Street (Box 4444) Crows Nest NSW 2065

First published 1988

National Library of Australia
Cataloguing-in-Publication entry
McCaughey, Davis,
Piecing together a shared vision.

Bibliography.
ISBN 0 642 53091 2.

1. Pluralism (Social sciences)—Australia.
2. Australia—Ethnic relations. 3. Australia—Social conditions. I. Australian Broadcasting Corporation.
II. Title. (Series 1 Boyer lectures; 1987).
305.8′00994

Edited by Jane Arms
Designed by Kim Roberts
Set in Garamond by Caxtons Pty Ltd, South Australia
Printed and bound in Australia by Australian Print Group, Victoria

Contents

I

Who Are We?

Thomas Davis, a great Irish patriot, wrote:

> This country of ours is no sand bank, thrown up by some recent caprice of earth. It is an ancient land, honoured in the archives of civilization, traceable into antiquity by its piety, its valour and its sufferings. Every great European race has sent its stream to the river of the Irish mind . . . If we live influenced by wind and sun and tree, and not by the passions and deeds of the past, we are a thriftless and a hopeless People.

Australia is not Ireland, and it would be easy to concentrate on the differences: the rhetoric of a 'sand bank thrown up by some recent caprice of earth' is inappropriate for this ancient land mass, millions of years old; and I doubt if we are 'honoured in the archives of civilization', least of all for our piety. Yet there are some haunting suggestions in those sentences.

First, what is our relation to 'wind and sun and tree'? Aboriginal peoples have made that—the earth, the land—the basis of their cultures. In the last 200 years a recognizable culture has appeared among pastoralists and those who have farmed the land: they know what it is to be conditioned by 'wind and sun and tree'. For all of us, in varying degree, Australian life is and has been concerned with the problem of holding on to this rim of earth, making what we can out of it, enjoying its fruits and surviving its disasters. In many ways this was an inhospitable country. If not simply 'wind and sun and trees', then drought and flood, fire and water, and the fluctuating price in the world's markets of our basic commodities have conditioned our lives. Survival has often been more important than anything else, whether on the beaches of Gallipoli or in the reduction of our national debt. In adversity we say that we live in an insecure, inhospitable, threatened country; when things go well we are a lucky country. One way or another we have not so much decided anything, we have had decisions made for us.

What I want to suggest in these lectures is that that is not a good enough way of looking at ourselves. The valour and sufferings of many peoples have contributed to our many-sided life. From the earliest days of Aboriginal cultures down to the arrival of the most recent group of refugees from South-East Asia, many peoples have contributed and are contributing to our common life—or could do so. If we neglect their past, we are neglecting our own past, we are a 'thriftless' people. If we simply allow decisions to be made for us, and do not face the future together, we shall be a 'hopeless' people. Maybe before we are finished we shall have a look again at the virtues of thrift and of hope. These may, more than we customarily recognize, be matters for decision: how we assess the past and how we face the future.

Meanwhile, who are we? and how do we get on together? Thomas Davis said that 'every great European race has sent its stream to the river of the Irish mind'. We can claim more. An Aboriginal culture, or rather Aboriginal cultures, Asian and Pacific as well as European peoples, have contributed to our life. In a different way from Ireland we have an ancient land, and if not *an* ancient civilization, then access to several ancient civilizations through the peoples who now live here. But please note that Thomas Davis spoke of how the rivers of many European cultures had fed the Irish *mind*. Never in the history of Australia have so many streams flowed: if we have parched and desiccated minds and spirits, the fault is our own. There is no reason why the judgements that we have to make on our various pasts, and our decisions about the future, should not be taken with informed minds. There is now no excuse for a conspiracy of silence, as it has been called, about our past. I may interject that that was a silence not only about how Aborigines were treated but also about the treatment of Irish and other immigrant groups. One example, however, of how that silence is being broken comes from the side of the victim in the recording of Aboriginal oral history. Over a whole series of issues, unless we break the silence, end the conspiracy unconsciously entered into by those with power, we cannot face the future with hope. There is nothing that engenders and nourishes fear like ignorance, and with it the threat to my status, my group, my understanding of the matter. To understand more fully who we are, what are the streams that go to make up our life, and to think hard about how we are to live, not merely survive together: that is a daunting agenda for the Australian people.

So far I have spoken as though Australian life has been constituted by successive waves of migrants, each bringing its own way of life, and learning to live upon and from this land in its own way. If, as we shall see, that is much too simple a way of seeing ourselves, it is nevertheless one of overwhelming importance just at present. There is no need to recall the history of immigration to Australia since the second world war. If we note that three million came here in little over thirty years, we have almost said it too fast: the very category 'migrant' disguises the complexity of the situation. Those three million belong to many different language groups, with different national backgrounds, different religious affiliations and different cultures. To take but one example: in 1947, in Victoria, there were only 16,000 people who professed a faith other than Christianity. Of these 94 per cent were Jews. By 1981 the total figure had risen to 90,000, only 41 per cent of whom were Jews. In Australia as a whole, the largest non-Christian group is Muslims. I would suppose that language and religion are two great cohesive forces holding together many groups in our community. With that go patterns of family life and varying attitudes to some social and moral questions.

It is no part of my intention to analyse again the multicultural nature of our society, or to trace again the varying attitudes towards, for instance, non-English speaking migrants implied in government policies and the attitudes of other Australians already settled in this country. I assume great diversity in what is infelicitously called 'ethnic background and origin'. I assume the importance of language and religion. I recognize the argument of 'a number of pioneers of cultural pluralism, that such a notion must inevitably lead to some degree of structural differentiation or "structural pluralism", and that multiculturalism should go beyond tolerance and diversity and recognize ethnic minorities as legitimate interest groups'. Then I want to ask, what is it that gives this society of ours cohesion? If it is not possible to ask yet about shared values, is it possible to speak about a shared vision? At this stage, I do not want to equate that with Professor Zubrzycki's 'dominant core culture with its English language, our judicial system and our English parliamentary institutions', which (he claims) can provide the foundation of the shared value of the freedom of the individual to pursue his or her private life. At the present stage of our discussion that may be too precise, claims a little too much, and yet is not broad enough. All I now want to do is to invite others to articulate for me, and with me, what meanwhile we may call 'a shared vision'.

Before we do so let us note another point about the diversity of groupings in our society. I introduce it by quoting from the *Review of the Australian Institute of Multicultural Affairs*. A contributor to that review notes that within a short period 'the understanding of the "migrant problem" had moved from a focus on settlement and assimilation to a focus on disadvantage'. In other words there were facts about some migrant groups that were, in the eyes of some members of the community, at least as important, perhaps more so than that they were Greeks or Italians or Yugoslavs or English or Irish. One of these facts was that many of them were poor. It was seen, to quote further, that 'factors external to the school system (such as race, sex, culture, class) handicapped children before they entered school'.

If we come at this from another angle, we might observe that what gives many Australians a sense of belonging, an identity, if you like, is not ethnic origin or national culture but a loyalty that over-rides such factors. Belonging to a union or a group of employers, playing football for a particular club, may be important in giving some people a sense of significance, either independently or along with other affiliations. In our day, for many, being a woman is the most important thing in their lives, and their solidarity with other women would over-ride what they believe to be lesser loyalties. Similarly, some men and women believe themselves to belong to the world of science and have a sense of solidarity with their fellow-scientists in other countries, which is to them more important than their membership of a particular nation, just as many Christians today sense that their membership of a worldwide church or fellowship of Christians is a transcending loyalty. In each case they, the scientists and the churchmen and women, may hope that the tension of which they are aware between themselves and their fellow-citizens will never reach the point at which there is a conflict of interests and loyalty; but in a world threatened by nuclear war they cannot be certain. There were conflicts from which some scientists and churchmen in Hitler's Germany or the Russia of Stalin were never able to escape. The state does not command our ultimate loyalty the way it once did.

Again, less worthily, some people in this community appear to be committed singlemindedly to the making of money, to making maximum profits, not necessarily, certainly not only for themselves, but also for the shareholders. If the taxation system works to their financial disadvantage, they will move their operations out of this country. The making of money is their culture. That is what gives their lives significance; and its pursuit—the pursuit of wealth—over-rules other considerations. At the other end of the scale are communes and the so-called drop-outs; but not all who call in question the values of an acquisitive society are properly so called. Many who are young, or who have been young in recent years, feel themselves to belong to a youth culture. They feel that they belong with, that they are understood better by their contemporaries than elsewhere, that they share a common culture expressed in each other's music, and that young people in other countries are more naturally their friends than some with whom they happen to be thrown together in their own country.

So we are a divided community, a much divided if not (or not yet) a deeply divided community: divided in our origins, our first language, our religion, and often in our ultimate loyalties. Not too much of this has been tested yet, to see how far it goes, how deeply it bites. I suppose that the Vietnam war disclosed some of the fissures in society; but for the most part we continue to live lives of some kind of conformity to the patterns around us. We tolerate each other, provided we do not come too close to one another. Nevertheless, the claims of the Aboriginal peoples remain at the back of our minds, the background of our lives and history, calling in question the easy acceptance of one another's ways: the test case, it is sometimes said, for a multicultural society.

Let us start then with the notion that we can live together provided we are a tolerant society. It is worth spending just a few minutes looking at the history and usages of that word, of that notion, tolerance.

Until the beginning of the eighteenth century, the word 'tolerance' had, certainly in French, a bad meaning: it suggested a lax complacency towards evil. It was one of the great achievements of the European Enlightenment of the eighteenth century to carry through a great reversal in the use of the word so that intolerance becomes a vice and tolerance a virtue. The most influential writing on the subject was by John Locke, an Englishman who wrote his famous *Letter on Toleration* in 1689. He wrote at the end of a century of religious strife in England, conflicts that were without precedent in English life and happily without successors. It was also a period marked by religious wars on the continent of Europe. What Locke was arguing for in the first place was freedom of religion, the right of diverse religious groups to worship in their own way. I imagine that most Australians would have little difficulty in going along with that. To gain something of its full force, however, let me read one of the few references to the rights of Jews in Locke's *Letter*:

> Indeed, to speak the truth, and as becomes one man to another, neither Pagan nor Mahometan nor Jew should be excluded from the commonwealth because of his religion. The Gospel commands no such thing. The church, which judges not them that are without, does not desire this. The commonwealth which receives and accepts men as men provided they are honest, peaceful and industrious, does not require it. Will you allow a Pagan to practise his trade in your country, but forbid him to pray to God or worship him? The Jews are permitted to have dwellings and private houses; why are they denied synagogues? . . . But if these things may be granted to Jews and Pagans, shall the condition of Christians in a Christian commonwealth be worse?

Locke is concerned, of course, with mutual toleration of Christians and uses the cases of Jews and others to reinforce his plea for such toleration. A principle is enunciated here, however, which, although it was not acted on for a hundred years or more, was to have far-reaching influence on liberal democratic thought. No man or woman should be excluded from society because of religious beliefs.

As I say, not many Australians would have difficulty with that. We have, after all, inherited partly from Locke and the Enlightenment a separation of church and state. The magistrate (as Locke called him) may not impose any rite or ceremony upon worshippers. Churches and other religious groups are free societies, or voluntary associations, which must settle their own forms of worship and doctrines.

Yet the matter is not quite so simple as that constitutional resolution would suggest. Some of the difficulties were foreseen by Locke himself.

First, anyone acquainted with the social history or literature of late seventeenth or early eighteenth-century Europe knows that Locke was asking much of his contemporaries. Maurice Cranston opens a noteworthy article on the subject with the words: 'Toleration is a policy of patient forbearance in the presence of something which is disliked or disapproved of.' It is not the same thing as indifference. It is more than belief in freedom of speech. I can defend freedom of speech without passing judgement on what might be said. But to tolerate means to some degree to pass a judgement: at least to say that I do not understand, perhaps to say that I dislike or even disapprove of the other party whose existence I tolerate. Not very many of us find it easy in practice to go the whole way with a remark attributed to Voltaire: 'I disapprove of what you say, but I will defend to the death your right to say it.' There are plenty of groups in Australia that would be happy to silence other groups.

The second reason why the exercise of tolerance is nothing like so simple as we at first thought is that there are limits to tolerance. We cannot tolerate the intolerant. Locke saw this. He excluded Roman Catholics and atheists from toleration. Roman Catholics were to be excluded because they owed allegiance to a foreign power (a not altogether unreasonable assumption at the end of the seventeenth century) and not on the whole because of their belief except (for instance) the teaching 'that faith may be broken with heretics', something that would undermine stable commercial relations. His objection to atheists was on the to us rather quaint grounds that oaths and promises would mean nothing to them. These he calls 'the bonds of human society'. We may deplore Locke's exceptions, but we must acknowledge that Locke recognized how fragile was the structure of human society, especially one dependent upon contracts and trade.

What Locke did assert, and it is important to return to it, is that the strong in society should not use their power against those who dissent unless their activities really were subversive; and I suppose that what we have come to see is that the majority, or the financially or politically strong, always have a tendency to define what is subversive as that which undermines their authority, their influence, the way *they* see things. A deeply held conviction about the value of tolerance needs to be widely spread among men and women who hold power. Here as elsewhere Acton's dictum holds: 'Power tends to corrupt. Absolute power corrupts absolutely.'

A third difficulty about tolerance is that, important though it is, the notion grew up in a world different from ours. Locke wrote against the background of an England that to some degree shared a common culture, and he was defending the right of the individual or the right of the group to organize his religious life within that context. Toleration had implied the recognition of the rights of people previously denied them, but they were people who already 'belonged' in that society: even though they had fought wars in the attempt to be dominant in that society.

The situation was different when groups previously either unrecognized or excluded or from afar came into Western society. What they sought was not merely tolerance but emancipation, a being set free to pursue their whole life and culture in a new context. The word 'emancipation' was first used in a widespread way of Catholic emancipation in Ireland and in England; it was used subsequently of Jewish emancipation throughout Europe; later again of the freeing of the slaves in North America; and then at the turn of the century of the emancipation of women. Heinrich Heine, the German poet born at the end of the eighteenth century, into 'an already strongly emancipated family of Jewish merchants', wrote in 1828 in quite heady terms of 'the great assignation of our times [as an] emancipation, not only of the people of Ireland, of the Greeks, of the Jews of Frankfurt, the blacks of West India and similar depressed peoples, but of the whole world, especially Europe'. What was being spoken of here was the arrival into Western society of whole groups in their cultural integrity and identity, now seeking a place in the sun previously denied them.

Locke had made two assumptions that no longer obtained for this new world. One was that society must tolerate what came to be known as a number of religious denominations: groups worshipping in different ways. The other was that when their legitimacy was recognized society would go on much as before, only more harmoniously. It was, however, quite different when emancipation hit the European and North American scene. An American writer has said of the Irish and the Jews that they were 'latecomers to modernity'; but we must notice that when they came they did not arrive simply as religious denominations. They arrived as people with their own culture, languages, ways of life. The Catholic Irish (but not only the Catholic Irish, some notable Protestant Irish also), the Jews of Eastern Europe (but not only of Eastern Europe), the blacks of North America and of the West Indies, women in the Western world (but not only in the Western world), have all come into the modern era as cultural groups, retaining something of their own identity and often with a language of their own. Moreover they have changed the world into which they have come. They have all shown what J.M. Cuddihy called 'a natural resistance to the current of assimilation'. Irish Catholics did not simply join a West British society when they achieved emancipation. They changed the character of Ireland, to some extent reviving an older culture suppressed but not destroyed, to some extent creating something new. And emancipated women rightly claim that they do not simply want to join a men's world when they are liberated and given equal opportunity. They want to change that world, bring to it some characteristically feminine attitudes and virtues.

We in Australia live this side of, and in the presence of, a number of these great emancipation movements. To some extent it is their presence that gives us some of the flavour of our common life. Perhaps the most striking of these is the effect of the Irish upon Australian life. I quote from Patrick O'Farrell's recently published *The Irish in Australia*. He writes about the nineteenth century:

> Whereas the smaller minorities—Germans, Italians—tended to be content with tolerance within a dominant British system, the Irish rejected or questioned the system, or at least demanded that it be adjusted to meet their requirements, with the effect of creating a new and modified system, a unique Australian blend and compromise, which fitted the character of a mixed and interacting group of people, on the basis of equity.

And again:

> The development of Australian nationalism can be seen, not as some wondrous and spontaneous outgrowth of climate and soil, pride and self-consciousness, but rather as a device invented and nurtured as a means of preventing an overwhelming growth of Englishness generated by the colonial governing classes. Again, not that the Irish held any monopoly of "Australian" views, but they were central to their championing, and conditioned Australia's cultural climate in such a way as to allow other deviations from Englishness to appear and flourish.

That is an interesting example of the effect of one emancipated group upon the structure and ethos of Australian society. If other groups are not to be content with tolerance we must expect similar contributions and changes to take place. If this is to happen creatively and not destructively, we must all be willing to receive changes gladly, if not uncritically; and to do so we must have some affirmative actions, some agreed frame of reference, and some way in which we prepare each other to live together, preserving the past—a thrifty people, and looking out to the future with hope. To our children and grandchildren we may then bequeath more than wind and sun and tree.

2

Something Beyond Ourselves

I should like to start by reading a few paragraphs by Alexander Solzhenitsyn:

> When you travel the by-roads of Central Russia you begin to understand the secret of the pacifying Russian countryside.
>
> It is in the churches. They trip up the slopes, ascend the high hills, come down to the broad rivers, like princesses in white and red, they lift their bell-towers—graceful, shapely, all different—high over mundane timber and thatch, they nod to each other from afar, from villages that are cut off and invisible to each other they soar to the same heaven. And wherever you wander in the fields or meadows, however far from habitation, you are never alone . . . some bell-tower will beckon to you.
>
> But when you get into the village you find that not the living but the dead greeted you from afar. The crosses were knocked off the roof or twisted out of place long ago. The dome has been stripped, and there are gaping holes between its rusty ribs. Weeds grow on the roofs and in the cracks in the walls . . . The murals over the altar have been washed by the rains of decades and obscene inscriptions written over them.
>
> People were always selfish and often unkind. But the evening chimes used to ring out, floating over villages, fields and woods. Reminding men that they must abandon the trivial concerns of this world and give time and thought to eternity. These chimes . . . raised people up and prevented them from sinking down on all fours.

Australia is not Russia. We have never had church bells ringing across the countryside. Wheat silos greet us from afar as we travel across the plains, and while necessary for our daily bread, they scarcely remind us of the trivial character of our daily concerns or point us to eternity. Yet none of the cultures from which we are sprung is without some witness to that which lies beyond the present. Those with a religious component could speak in terms not too far distant from Solzhenitsyn. Those with a humanist bent can speak of hopes and fears beyond present necessities. Almost all would concede that there is more to life than lubricating oil, the film show at six and dancing at eight o'clock: according to Solzhenitsyn the use to which many churches in Russia were then put.

Is that 'more', however, anything which we have in common?

In speaking about a shared vision in this country we cannot do so in terms of ultimate truths. It is easy to see how a shared vision can be presented, even required of citizens, in a totalitarian country such as Iran, or one in which there is an official ideology such as Soviet Russia. Marxism has provided a philosophy of history based on ultimate convictions about human nature on which a number of regimes have been able to build their hopes and expectations. In Australia men and women certainly have ultimate convictions, but they are not shared, nor can they be required of every member of the community: they are embedded in religious convictions, in cultural traditions, in philosophies of life that differ considerably.

Our 'shared vision' needs to be about things that we can hold in common although based on different premises, on fundamental convictions that may appear to be inconsistent one with another or even in conflict. There are, however, some penultimate convictions that we can hold in common.

Let me try to make a little clearer what I mean by the penultimate. I take an example used by Dietrich Bonhoeffer. He says: 'When I am with someone who has suffered a bereavement, I often decide to adopt a "penultimate" attitude . . . remaining silent as a sign that I share in the bereaved man's helplessness in the face of such a grievous event, and not speaking the biblical words of comfort which are, in fact, known to me and available to me.' He goes on to show, I think, that this is not a compromise with the truth. 'Account must be taken of people as they are,' he says. 'The ultimate remains totally on the far side of the everyday.'

In these lectures we shall try to think of people where they are in a multicultural, very diverse society, where the ultimate questions about life and death remain on the far side of the everyday reality that we share. I do not mean that these ultimate words are irrelevant to our everyday world; but they remain on the far side of the everyday reality *that we share*. If the ultimate questions are, so to speak, on the far side of the shared vision of which we could speak, specific policies are on this side: they are right in the foreground. What we are talking about is a middle ground on which we can stand together, even though we differ on fundamental convictions and on political policies to be pursued. All societies need some degree of consensus on this middle ground. I would like to discuss what we in Australia need, not simply describe what we may or may not have.

I suggest that we need a vision of something beyond our immediate interests. We might begin by asking, are there things that we must regard as sacred? More often than not we use that word negatively. We say of the cynical self-seeking man that apparently nothing to him is sacred: there is nothing that he will not do, no sacrifice of the well-being of others that he will not make, to further his own ends. Of those who make themselves wealthy and powerful through organized crime, by destroying the lives of others through drugs and corruption, we say that to them nothing seems to be sacred.

More positively there are areas in the lives and cultures of various groups in Australia that we should respect because they are sacred to those groups (and from which the rest of us might learn), and there are areas that we must all regard as sacred if we are to have a shared vision.

Of the first category—things, places, customs that are sacred to particular groups—we think most readily of the Aborigines. To live in a multicultural Australia certainly involves a respect for their claims to land, their sacred sites, and their attitude towards the environment, which is strange to many of us who are not of Aboriginal descent. Most of us will never fully understand, a few will obtain glimpses into the lives and cultures of others, which will help the rest of us. Nevertheless many of us can go further in understanding than we do. It must not be an antiquarian interest, a mere curiosity about how others live. It must reach an awareness at a fairly deep level of self-consciousness of our common humanity.

Did we not know their blood channelled our rivers,
and the black dust our crops ate was their dust?
O all men are one man at last. We should have known
the night that tided up the cliffs and hid them
had the same question on its tongue for us.
And there they lie that were ourselves writ strange.

So Judith Wright.

Out of that encounter with Aboriginal culture, however difficult to understand in our terms, come two things essential for our shared vision. The first is our common humanity, in its diverse manifestations, not to be regarded as threat or promise, but as part of the essential data of our lives. We have to learn to stand before our fellowman and woman with humility.

Let me try to develop that just a little. One of the most persistent tendencies apparent among men and women with power over others is to try to make those others like themselves. This urge is particularly strong if the powerful—those who have something to give—see the others as weak, or of lower intelligence or of lesser technical achievement than themselves. The history of military conquest, of the attempts by one nation or empire to dominate another is full of such instances. So is the story of those of us who are lesser teachers. It is easier, much easier, to try to process students than it is to introduce them to what is worth thinking about, and to teach them to think. So, too, when we meet other cultural groups, whether they are of Aboriginal origin or of another language group from a national background other than our own, our natural tendency is to want to assimilate them to our way of doing things.

It would now be widely agreed that assimilation is a poor notion of how an older culture should be related to that of the white settlers; and that it is equally inappropriate to speak of the assimilation of, for instance, non-English speaking migrants to our English language-based culture. In the first lecture I tried to suggest that the process of emancipation, of finding a new freedom in a new land, which has been the experience of many migrant groups, will not leave us unchanged. An awareness of that comes to many as threat: we do not enjoy being changed. It is seen by others as promise: a future in which the lion will lie down with the lamb. If we have to choose between the two, it is much better to live under a promise of richer better things than under threat; and in the end a shared vision must be a vision of the future, preferably filled with hope rather than foreboding. What at this stage I am trying to suggest is that before we settle for either threat or promise, we pause and learn what it is to view our neighbour with respect, I was going to say, with reverence. I once used that word in the presence of Michael Polanyi, the distinguished chemist and philosopher, and to my relief he approved. 'I sometimes tell my students,' he said 'that there are some substances which you can only see by use of a microscope, and others with the help of a telescope; but you can see greatness through reverence.' The word 'reverence' is appropriate when we are asking: can the sense of the sacred be a part of our shared vision?

Out of our encounter with Aboriginal culture, or cultures, there come two things essential to our shared vision. One was a sharp reminder, in Judith Wright's words, that 'all men are one man at last'. The second is that the story of the Aborigines' encounter with the land brings before us in vivid terms the relation between tool-making man and the environment that surrounds him and from which he wrests his livelihood. In both these there are at least 'intimations' of the sacred: 'there they lie that were ourselves writ strange'.

The cluster of questions to do with the preservation and conservation of the environment has its roots in the Aborigines' past. As Professor Geoffrey Blainey, Professor John Mulvaney and other historians have shown, there are continuous as well as broken threads between the ancient and recent history of Australia; and while historical events do not repeat themselves—there is an almost infinite variation in the ways in which men and women live with, live from, use and exploit their environment—we surely need to learn, and that quickly, how to live with respect for our environment if we are to survive. Meanwhile that respect may teach us some reverence, which is an end in itself.

The new sense of the sacred, stated in penultimate terms, is a task for us all. There are things that as a community we will not do, whatever the cost of that refusal. Positively we would preserve critical areas of our heritage: for instance, we should never destroy the Great Barrier Reef whatever the financial inducements; we should also seek to preserve for our fellow man the integrity of his culture.

I want now to turn to another area in which this claim may and should be heard. To put it in a phrase, the claim should be heard and acknowledged in the intellectual life of the nation.

An Irish historian recently wrote: 'To the Irish all history is applied history, and the past is simply a convenient quarry which provides ammunition to use against enemies in the present. They have little interest in it for its own sake.'

That is a terrible indictment. It suggests that it is not the truth of the matter that is sacred, only the use to which the material may be put. Of course, it is well known that all history is written or perceived from a particular point of view. The past is always appreciated in a particular perspective: one age may chiefly be interested in its past as the story of constitutional arrangements, of the history of government, or of art or of thought. The past may make its impact upon us in a score of different ways. You remember Wordsworth's 'Solitary Highland Lass'?:

A voice so thrilling ne'er was heard
In spring-time from the Cuckoo-bird,
Breaking the silence of the seas
Among the farthest Hebrides.

Will no one tell me what she sings?—
Perhaps the plaintive numbers flow
For old, unhappy, far-off things,
And battles long ago:
Or is it some more humble lay,
Familiar matter of today?
Some natural sorrow, loss, or pain
That has been, and may be again?

Recent historians have asked us to look at the past from the bottom upwards; they say: not the story of kings and how they reigned but of ordinary people and how their lives were lived and changed.

The perspective of different historians may be conditioned by class interest, or by some psychological factor: Marx and Freud have done their work well in disclosing to us the interests that we try to conceal from ourselves, and from other people. What somebody called the vulgar sociology of knowledge question, *Who* says that? may always be asked. But that only means that the more viewpoints we have upon our past the better. It does not mean that the past is not worth studying for its own sake. There is all the difference in the world between, on the one hand, knowing that your knowledge is partial and, on the other, using the past as a quarry from which to build a secure house for yourself in the present. There is all the difference between acknowledging that you have a limited personal view and selecting the data that suits you for propaganda purposes. The teaching of history must not be a technique for processing students into one viewpoint, but of setting them free to be interested in the past from a variety of points of view but for its own sake. As with the environment, we must avoid exploiting the past and treat it with respect.

The same quality to which we have alluded is needed here, namely humility before the past and humility about our own capacity to set the record straight. The rediscovery of the past and its significance is never finished. If, as we must, we apply this to multicultural, pluralist Australia, we have much to learn from each other, from the oral history of Aboriginal tribal life, from those who see our history and development through eyes that have worn continental European and Asian glasses as well as those manufactured in the United Kingdom and Ireland. To all the truth of the matter must be sacred, even though we shall never attain it.

There is an almost exact parallel to this in our attitude to science. I sometimes fear that a future historian will write: 'To the Australians of the closing decades of the twentieth century all science was applied science, and scientific enquiry became simply a convenient quarry that provided ammunition to use for commercial and industrial purposes. They had little interest in it for its own sake.' If that can be said, then a serious denigration of our cultural heritage will have occurred. Science will have ceased to be wisdom and become only power; for like art and religion science speaks of the human race's endless search for wisdom. It is not concerned primarily about how power may be exercised or enhanced, although that is part of its story.

Just as the study of history for its own sake provides a knowledge of the past that will help us to understand better who and what we are in the present, so, too, science normally has had, and is likely always to have, an edge, cutting into men and women's present-day concerns. It does put power into our hands; but the edge will only cut if we care about the truth of the matter. The scientific education that most students have received in the universities of the Western world over the past one hundred and fifty or even two or three hundred years has been important because it has taught men and women the experimental method and how to think scientifically. It has done this in a variety of disciplines, which the graduates may or may not have pursued in their subsequent careers. It was the approach rather than the application that mattered and that has enriched them and our society. And, of course, it has been demonstrated over and over again that basic scientific discoveries result in, are essential to, developments in applied science and technology. Applied science and technology need the rigour and self-criticism of the scientific method every bit as much as do the basic sciences on which they depend.

As in the study of history, so scientific enquiry has rarely been free of presuppositions and biases. We are all conditioned creatures, and no one knows quite what motives are at work in urging us to undertake enquiries in this field or that. Nevertheless, at its heart, the agenda for scientific enquiry has normally been set by the next right question to ask, given the present state of the art. In other words, scientific enquiry has been undertaken in large measure for its own sake; a wise country will see that its scientists continue to pursue their enquiries in this spirit. The truth is sacred, and even though here (as in the study of history) there are no final solutions, the man or woman of science must be free to ask the next right question and to hold him or herself responsible to the world of science, which alone is in the position to judge the validity of the enquiry. The community of scientists has in the last century or more developed an intricate series of checks whereby the integrity of various scientific enquiries is tested. Journals with articles that have been approved for publication by experts in the field, learned bodies, academies of scientists, maintain a watching brief upon the development of different scientific disciplines. A wise community will not expect its legislators to step in and define the limits of enquiry, except when they are manifestly a threat to human life or to the environment. Freedom of enquiry is as essential to the man or woman of science as freedom of worship to the man or woman of faith; and the two may not be far apart.

One hundred years ago modern science had to fight to keep itself free from the control of religiously formulated propositions about nature and the origins of life, just as in previous decades universities had to free themselves from ecclesiastical control. The threat does not come from those quarters today, certainly not in Australia. The threat comes from a society that wants all learning to be helpful immediately in the solution of problems understood in short runs. We are told that education must be relevant; but to what? Relevant to showing men and women that there are things worth pursuing for their own sake, that man's chief and most important characteristic is an attitude of something akin to reverence, certainly awe before what he does and does not know.

One reason why it is important to stress the importance of science as part of the human person's search for wisdom is that many people do not understand the distinction between science and technology. Most of us see the results, for better or for worse, of the application of science. We can see all around us a world changed by technology. Few of us see, or understand, what goes on in a scientific laboratory or what is involved in a scientific enquiry. It is probably unobtrusive, and it involves asking questions, many of which will not be answered in terms that are applicable to any urgent problem with which we are confronted today, although in the long term they may be extremely important. Meanwhile they are a part of the wisdom of the race.

Michael Polanyi draws attention to the different vocabulary we use, and rightly use, with relation to science and technology. Science speaks in indicatives: the past, the present, the future—what has been, what is, and what perhaps will be. Technology speaks in imperatives: what must be done to make things work. Science is more closely related to knowledge, where the suggestion may be true or false, while technology is closer to action, and 'action can only be unsuccessful or successful, right or wrong'. Science looks for discoveries, technology for inventions. To quote Polanyi:

> The beauty of an invention differs from the beauty of a scientific discovery. Originality is appreciated in both, but in science originality lies in the power of seeing more deeply than others into the nature of things, while in technology it consists in the ingenuity of the artificer in turning known facts to a surprising advantage.

We do not need to lose either of these approaches, which have become such an important part of the life of the human race in the twentieth century. We must always seek to maintain a balance: applied science, technology, is certainly transforming the world; but the chief motive of science is to understand the world. What is under threat today is not technological development: it may be suffering from neglect, but it is believed to be important. What is under threat is science. It may easily be entering a period of something worse than neglect, namely of being undervalued.

In most parts of the world politicians are more interested in technology than in science. They are men and women of action and they want to see things done. Few of them have had anything more than a rudimentary education in science, or give the impression of having any love for it. They fall easily to the blandishments of the technocrats of an industrial society. The most extreme example of this is the ideological utilitarianism of a number of Soviet governments; but extremes meet and from right as from left the demand is made that universities and research institutes should simply serve the nation's needs. Love of science is sometimes regarded as an indulgence that we cannot afford. Knowledge is much less important than action. This is understandable but dangerous. The same people who today control the money needed for basic research are those who must (have been asked by society to) solve short-term problems. One can understand their impatience but deplore it.

'No important discovery' says Polanyi 'can be made in science by anyone who does not believe that science is important—indeed supremely important—in itself.'

So we are back to where we have been before: nothing that is really important will be done except by people who believe in it. You cannot apply cost-benefit analysis to the assertion that other members of the human race are precious, that the environment should be respected, that you should not tamper with historical knowledge, that you should value scientific understanding of the world around you. These things do provide men and women with a richer life. They are in their way sacred, and as such must be a part of our shared vision.

3

Professions and Conventions: *a matter of trust.*

Readers of Charles Dickens's *Bleak House* will remember his satirical account of the legal profession:

The one great principle of the English law is to make business for itself. There is no other principle distinctly, certainly, and consistently maintained through all its narrow turnings. Viewed by this light it becomes a coherent scheme, and not the monstrous maze the laity are apt to think. Let them but once clearly perceive that its grand principle is to make business for itself at their expense, and surely they will cease to grumble.

If Dickens takes on the law, George Eliot in *Middlemarch* exposes the medical profession with some beautiful shafts of irony, and Trollope has contributed to the popular imagination—through his Barchester novels mediated recently by television—the figures of Archdeacon Grantley and Mr Slope, not to mention the Bishop and Mrs Proudie. Those three instances suggest that in the last century something more was expected of the three so-called learned professions, law, medicine, the church, than self-seeking or the perpetuation of the institution to the advantage of its chief practitioners.

It is important to notice in each case that the authors concerned are being satirical or employing irony. They are not giving a cynical account of these three professions, much less are they describing them literally. Satire implies a norm from which this description is a deviation; irony sets out to deflate social pretentions. If it were not usual to claim something better than this for, say, the legal profession, Dickens's writing would lose much of its force. When I showed the passage from Dickens to a lawyer friend, he said that he would like to balance the ledger by referring me to a quotation from Edmund Burke:

> The study of the law renders men acute, inquisitive, dexterous, prompt in attack, ready in defence, full of resources. Lawyers argue misgovernment at a distance, and snuff the approach of tyranny in every tainted breeze.

It is, of course, precisely to deflate that kind of pomposity that Dickens writes as he does; but behind Dickens's satire is the assumption that there should be, is intended to be, a better way of ordering things.

We live in a period in which traditional institutions have lost something of the respect they once had. Dr Johnson distinguished between a satire and a lampoon. The former, satire, censures wickedness or folly; the latter, the lampoon, originally a drinking song, is simply a violent attack upon an individual. The satire has a serious social purpose: it would reform behaviour. It is therefore almost something of a compliment when a profession is the subject of satire: it suggests that people still expect something better of it. When individual members, perhaps representing a profession, are the subject of lampoons, we have reached the stage when we no longer expect anything of them. When we reach the stage of cynicism in which we suspect everything that members of a profession do as being entirely self-interested and proceed on that assumption, then the possibility of trust is excluded from our attitude to them.

If my earlier chapter was about humility, this one is about trust. I want to suggest that we need to be able to trust our institutions and the professional men and women who run them; but that they, in turn, need to be trustworthy. In doing this, I am asking that our shared vision of a better society is one which must be diffused among different professions and occupations in the community. I shall confine myself to references to members of the professions, because they have certain definable characteristics and responsibilities.

Let me explain a little further what I mean by a diffused vision; and I shall do so with reference to an interesting shift in the way in which many in all the churches have come to think about themselves. It is a shift that has parallels in secular society.

When I was young and first interested in theological and

ecclesiastical affairs, there was much discussion—and had been for some time, some of it very heated—about the place of bishops and presbyters in the life of the church, never to mention the papacy. From about the time of the Oxford Movement in the Church of England, Anglicans, for instance, had become very interested in episcopacy and the apostolic succession, and so on. Other denominations responded, rather like 'Annie Get Your Gun', by singing, 'I can do anything better than you.' Now, no doubt, these are serious matters: the hierarchical structure of the church is in some ways either essential or very important to its life. But the focus has changed. It has changed not simply to a greater attention being given to the laity, which is something of an abstraction. Attention is now focused on Paul's understanding of the church, as a body with many members; and those members have different gifts and callings. It would be a false view of the church, just as it would be a false view of society, to say that anybody can do anything. What the apostle Paul said was that everybody can do something.

Other ancient writers and thinkers used this metaphor of the body to represent the body politic or the cosmos: a body with members. No one, so far as I know, developed it in quite the same way as Paul, seeing the members as each having a different vocation and with the appended warning that one part of the body should not think of itself more highly or look down upon another apparently lesser part. Each needed the other.

Similarly we are just beginning to see a new approach to moral questions. We are not only interested in the moral behaviour of individuals or in the standards accepted by society as a whole. The individual and society as a whole is a false dichotomy. We all belong to a variety of societies, our family, our neighbourhood, our professional or occupational group, those with whom we share a cultural background or a religious faith. The conventions that control the behaviour of different groups within society are of interest. Among these, we are hearing more of professional ethics, that is, of the codes, conventions, guidelines that control the patterns of life adopted by members of a profession. For the moment do not let us trouble ourselves with the question, where do professions end and other types of activity begin. Almost certainly the areas in which a genuine professionalism is being developed are widening all the time. That's a good thing. Doctors, parsons and lawyers have no monopoly on behaving in a professional manner; but it is equally true that not every association can or needs to be regarded as a profession in order to have important functions to perform in society, functions that must be performed in an ethical manner. Certain kinds of service, however, carry with them obligations that we have come to regard as characteristically professional.

An American writer has suggested that it is the fusing of three values in a profession which gains other people's respect. First, 'the value placed upon systematic knowledge and the intellect: knowing. Second the value placed upon technical skill and trained capacity: doing. And third, the value placed upon putting this conjoint knowledge and skill to work in the service of others: helping'. Let me repeat: it is the fusion of these three—knowing, doing, helping—that gains the respect of clients and of the community. In placing value first upon systematic knowledge and the intellect, it is implied that training and technical competence are not enough. We expect, or should expect, members of the professions that serve us to be intellectuals: our lawyers to have an awareness of the history of law and the place of law in our society, our doctors to think scientifically and not just treat symptoms, executive officers of enterprises public and private to be capable of referring to fundamental principles of management and to be aware of the assumptions about human nature made in those principles, clergy to be theologically competent. And we expect, or should expect, of members of professions that because they place value on this systematic knowledge, this activity of the intellect, they will be self-critical. Only on the base of a humble intellectualism will the necessary skills be developed and appropriate action taken so that the members of professions can really help. Lots of people can and should care for each other in the community. There is always the need for a kindly neighbour. But from members of a profession we expect more: we expect a reflective and technically skilful meeting of our needs—what A.D. Lindsay called the scientific mind in the service of the merciful heart.

There is one more thing to be said about the professionals' responsibility to know: the knowing to which he or she is committed is not just intellectual, it has a moral content. The true professional serves a cause even greater than the need of his or her individual patient or client. In the case of the physician that cause is the promotion of health and the alleviation of suffering. In the case of the lawyer that cause is the cause of justice. 'It is a universal rule of conduct for all lawyers,' writes one of them, 'that they must never knowingly be parties to the deception of a court, however much good that might do for their clients.' Or to quote a great judicial statement of the nineteenth century:

He [the advocate] is a representative but not a delegate. He gives to his client the benefit of his learning, his talents and his judgement; but all through he never forgets what he owes to himself and to others. He will not knowingly mistate the law, he will not wilfully mistate the facts, though it be to gain the cause for his client. He will ever bear in mind that if he be the advocate of an individual, and *retained* and remunerated (often inadequately) for his valuable services, yet he has a prior and perpetual *retainer* on behalf of truth and justice; and there is no Crown or other licence which in any case, or for any party or purpose, can discharge him from that primary and paramount retainer.'

Having heard that we can now turn to the third element in the professional's commitment, namely to help. The true professional has a transcending loyalty to something greater than the interest of his patient or client: that is his paramount commitment. But the second is like to it: he must always prefer the client or patient's interest to his own. That sounds easy; but it is not always so because there is normally what has been called 'a gross inequality of power' between the professional and the one he helps or serves. We go for help to professionals because they know more than we do; and in this relationship knowledge is power. In the exercise of that power the professional is to his client in what Titmuss called 'a gift relationship'. 'The cardinal sin of any professional,' it has been said, 'and the prime ground for his expulsion from the profession, is to prefer his own interest to that of his patient or client.' It should never be able to be said of the professional that he is in it for what he can get out of it. He or she is there with something to give—mostly advice, but at all events a service. He is not in the market-place to obtain the highest possible price for his commodity; and the scarcer the commodity the higher the price that it can command. Hence there grew up a tradition that the remuneration received by a member of a profession should be sufficient to relieve him from financial anxiety and to enable him to live in reasonable comfort and cultivation, but that membership of a profession should not be thought of as a way in which to amass considerable wealth. No doubt there have always been some wealthy doctors and some wealthy lawyers, but for most the question has been: have they enough? And what is enough? The wisdom literature of Israel defined that a long time ago:

Give me neither poverty nor riches;
feed me with the food that is needful for me,
lest I be full, and deny thee,
and say, 'Who is the Lord?'
or lest I be poor, and steal,
and profane the name of my God.

This runs counter to some strong tendencies in our society. John Nieuwenhuysen and Marina Williams-Wynn introduce their valuable study of four professions in Australia with a quotation from Adam Smith:

> We trust our health to the physician, our fortune and sometimes our life and reputation to the lawyer and attorney. Such confidence could not safely be reposed in people of a very low or mean condition. Their reward must be such, therefore, as may give them that rank in society which so important a trust requires.

There are other more contemporary writers who suggest that a member of a profession must look prosperous, otherwise we would not trust him. The opposite tendency—namely the appearance, if not the reality, of an excessive prosperity—creates at least equally great problems. When professional associations appear before the public as more concerned about financial rewards than about the standards of their practice, when they appoint what they call 'industrial officers' and take what is called 'industrial action', then something has gone seriously wrong not only in the professions but also with our society.

Another traditional assumption made about members of a profession is that they will not indulge in nepotism, that is to say, in the promotion of the interests of a relative or friend beyond that of another better or equally qualified candidate. Bias arising from family links or friendship should be eliminated. No doubt it has always been easier for a member of a well-known legal or medical family to get started in his profession, no doubt class distinction has reared its ugly head in the selection of some for appointment or promotion over others. But in principle, at least, and generally in practice, nepotism or preference based upon a candidate's family connection, or the school to which he or she went, or whether he be a man or woman, or a member of this race or that, would be regarded as improper. There *are*, however, societies and cultures in which the promotion of the interests of members of your own family is regarded as the over-riding duty, the supreme virtue.

Conflicts can arise when such cultures come into contact with what I can only call Western professionalism. In Australia we must insist that the traditional standards of that professionalism prevail; but we must make sure that our own houses are in order.

How are these high standards to be maintained? Dr Nieuwenhuysen and Miss Williams-Wynn discuss at some length the ways in which four professions—law, medicine, accounting and dentistry—might be brought within existing legislation, especially on advertising and remuneration. Members of professions have customarily been under legal restraints of one kind or another, and those restraints no doubt need to be re-defined again and again. What I am arguing for here goes further than that: it asks for a greater trust in each other's activities and for greater trustworthiness on the part of professions in society in particular. You cannot legislate for trust. You can only penalize those who betray trust. You cannot make lawyers or teachers or doctors good by Act of Parliament. You can scarcely do more than stop them being excessively wicked, acting to the detriment of other members of society. For centuries many English speaking Christians have prayed each Sunday for those that are put in authority under the sovereign 'that they may truly and impartially administer justice, to the punishment of wickedness and vice, and to the maintenance of true religion and virtue'.

The first part of that indicates very clearly the limits of the law, the punishment of wickedness and vice. The maintenance of true religion and virtue has very largely been handed over to other people. The best chance of improving quality of performance rests with the professions themselves and (as we shall see) with interested members of the community. Under peer pressure better standards of behaviour may be achieved because without it there can be trust neither between members of the profession itself, nor between professions and society. Even Lord Devlin, who thought that the law could do more to enforce morality than most of his colleagues would allow, put the matter pungently:

> The criminal law is not a statement of how people ought to behave; it is a statement of what will happen to them if they do not behave; good citizens are not expected to come within reach of it or set their sights by it, and every enactment should be framed accordingly.

Good citizens will not only avoid doing what the law prohibits, they will do what the law as such does not have in view. They will not wish to test the limits of the admissible; for to do justly and to act rightly is to act in ways well this side of the law. The good citizen does not simply see how far he may go.

Let me take an example, which may not be acceptable to all but raises some questions. It is no part of the responsibility of the good accountant, or lawyer, to tell his client how far he may go in avoiding taxation if he knows that all the time he is simply encouraging the evasion of taxation: he has found a loophole through existing legislation. The rest of us would hope that there are some firms of accountants and lawyers who simply will not handle that kind of business. We rely on societies of accountants and institutes of lawyers to put pressure on their members to speak for restraint by their clients in their conduct of affairs well short of that point at which their activities become actionable before the law. Similarly we should not need laws to prohibit every imaginable unacceptable practice by doctors or medical scientists. The professions themselves, or public bodies acting on their behalf, should point to a better way. Professional bodies can be tough with their own members, and frequently are so. I read recently a code of business ethics observed for many years by a large American business house. It ends by saying: 'It is difficult to imagine field violation of our code which would not constitute grounds for dismissal of anyone involved.'

It is, however, quite unrealistic to expect many members of a profession to act in better ways than do most, unless they are provided with guidance from the profession itself. Wise legislators will leave a high degree of this guidance to the professions. What Polanyi says about wider aspects of our society applies here also:

> The recognition granted in a free society to the independent growth of science, art and morality involves a dedication of society to the fostering of a specific tradition of thought, transmitted and cultivated by a particular group of authoritative specialists, perpetuating themselves by co-option.

Many will object to that. Men and women, they will say, are not to be trusted with the ordering of their own affairs: medical science is too far-reaching in its implications for mankind to be left to the scientists, biotechnology too frightening in its claims to be left to the biologists, just as nuclear physics has put power into men's hands too devastating to be left to the physicists. The twentieth century has seen some very nasty cases of the misuse of information and position by members of professions, as well as some brave attempts to obstruct corruption. There have been and are some matters on which professional people have to be restrained by law. Otherwise law and justice and compassion are themselves damaged. Members of professions have sometimes not only been self-seeking, they have co-operated on schemes to break the law and have left themselves open to criminal charges. Society by means of legislation protects itself against malpractice. The law has an essential part to play here in the restraint of wickedness. But in 'the fostering of a specific tradition of thought' or ethic, its transmission and cultivation, we depend to a high degree on specialists who must not allow themselves to be edged out of taking responsibility because they are accused of being an elite.

It is not clear that outsiders always do see more of the game than those playing it. It is not clear that social scientists and bureaucrats, or political bodies whose members have been elected because they have other skills, would be better than members of professions in seeing where and how restrictions can reasonably be put on their members. For the punishment of wickedness, yes; but for the promotion of virtue, no! We live in a society, however, when it has been widely recognized that the choice is not simply between men and women regulating their own affairs, each generation of scientists or lawyers, each individual practitioner making up his or her own mind. We never have been without conventions that control our actions. We all belong to societies, social groupings—the family, gender, the locality, our profession, our trade, political groupings, our membership of the human race—which are governed by conventions. 'Much of the work of the world,' notes Professor Dorothy Emmet, 'and the stability of any society depends on the routine practice of the functional morality of "my station and its duties", which is codified in law and custom.' Of these two, custom, or convention, is far more important than law in giving our society cohesion.

Custom, that unwritten law,
By which the people keep even kings in awe.

What we have seen with increasing frequency in the twentieth century is the codification of those conventions into Conventions with a capital 'C'. These sometimes have international significance—the Helsinki Declaration on Human Experimentation adopted by the eighteenth World Medical Assembly in 1964, is but one of many examples—or have force only within a nation. More and more professions are seeing the need for such guidance for their members: nurses and social workers are relative newcomers in this respect, groups that are laying down ethical guidelines for their members.

One very important development in this respect has been the increasing tendency of members of professions to invite others to consult with them in the drafting of such guidelines. In this country the medical profession, and medical scientists in particular, have been foremost in doing just that. Confronted by questions of far-reaching ethical and human import they have invited men and women of other disciplines, with different experiences of community life, to join them in facing those questions. That is the right way round. We must not remove the responsibility for moral action from those who operate within a certain sphere, whether that is medicine, law, social work, accountancy, business management; but we may expect members of those professions to reach decisions in consultation with those whom they serve, as patients, as clients, as members of the community. I personally have had some experience of such wider consultation in the last six years working with others on the Medical Research Ethics Committee of the National Health Medical Research Council, of which committee more than half the members are not medically trained. The acceptance of guidelines, drafted by that committee and adopted by the council, by research workers and practitioners in hospitals and research institutes throughout the country is an example of the enhancement of moral responsibility within a particular profession, which we must seek if professions are to be trusted and to become increasingly trustworthy. I quote Professor Dorothy Emmet again:

> It is surely no evasion of the moral responsibility of the individual to ask that some lines may be laid down for his guidance in some of the more typically recurrent problems and temptations which he will meet in his professional roles. For it is abundantly clear that this will not mean that his own powers of moral judgement need go unexercised.

An exercise of moral responsibility diffused throughout the community, expressed in terms applicable to a variety of professions and occupations, is a part of the shared vision that we should have for our society.

4

Ourselves Writ Strange

George Eliot wrote:

A human life should be well rooted in some spot of a native land, where it may get the love of tender kinship for the face of the earth, for the labours men go forth to, for the sounds and accents that haunt it, for whatever will give that early home a familiar unmistakable difference amidst the future widening of knowledge: a spot where the definiteness of early memories . . . may spread not by sentimental effort and reflection, but as a sweet habit of the blood.

That was in 1876, and George Eliot was writing in England. Over a century later, we live at the end of a sixty or seventy-year period in which we have experienced one of the most massive movements of population, from one part of the world to another, of men and women of one culture coming in contact with another, that the world has ever seen. For millions of people it is no longer possible for 'a human life' to be 'well rooted in some spot of a native land', 'the love of tender kinship for the face of the earth' is no longer open to them, 'the labours to which men go forth' are no longer the accustomed ones, and the early memories of many could scarcely be described as 'a sweet habit of the blood'. Moreover this is Australia. This has become for many the end of that massive movement of population. This is not the place of an early home which has for them 'a familiar unmistakable difference amidst the future widening of knowledge'. They look back and they look elsewhere. They are Greeks or Yugoslavs or Italians or Irish or English, Vietnamese or Chinese, but now for them not that distant land but Australia, the new land, is home.

Yet, they have come bringing with them the culture of another land and place, and the experience of being separated from the familiar things that once made them at home there. I suggested earlier that we can only understand our present life here if we recognize that many groups in this society have the characteristics of 'emancipated' groups: they have come to Australia certainly to start again, not as individuals to be assimilated into traditional Australian ways (if such exist), but as cultural entities. This situation is one which is potentially enriching. There are resources among us which could enable our children and our grandchildren to be among the most perceptive and cultivated people of the twenty-first century—if we do not throw away the opportunity. It is going to require effort.

In the second and third chapters, I suggested that we need to acquire a new humility before our neighbours, our environment and before what we do not know; and that we must learn to trust, and to make trustworthy, the institutions within which we work. Now I want to speak of the need to acquire and value more highly the languages and the literature in which the diverse cultures have come to us, and I want to go beyond that which is represented by migrant groups among us to speak of the danger of losing from our memories and imagination the great stories of mankind. 'The characteristic danger of great nations, like the Romans or the English,' wrote Walter Bagehot, 'which have a long history of continuous creation, is that they may at last fail from not comprehending the great institutions they have created.' That applies to the languages, the literature, the art and the music of a people, and of peoples, as it does of the institutions of government, of the law, of commerce and of science.

First, the learning of languages. There is no quicker way of depriving a people of its identity, of diminishing its dignity, than by taking away its language, and imposing upon it the language of the conqueror. John Dunmore Lang in 1824 deplored the way in which Aboriginal names were ignored and the name of the colonial administrator imposed:

Twas said of Greece two thousand years ago,
That every stone i' the land had got a name.
Of New South Wales too, men will soon say so;
But every stone there seems to get the same.
'Macquarie' for a name is all *the go*:
The old Scotch Governor was fond of fame.

Macquarie Street, Place, Port, Fort, Town, Lake, River:
'Lachlan Macquarie, Esquire, Governor', for ever!

He goes on to express his love of Aboriginal names, of Parramatta, and Illawarra and twenty more; and suggests that if names are introduced let them be of those who have stood for freedom in the annals of mankind. Names matter.

But more than names: if we are to see life through the eyes of others, we must learn something of their languages; and it is difficult to see that there is something in the genes of English-speaking Australians that makes it more difficult for them than for other comparable people to speak more than one language. Yet our record is bad; and in some respects is worse than was once the case. A submission made by linguists from the Australian National University to the federal government recently suggests that barely fifty of the two hundred Aboriginal languages that existed before 1788 are still being passed on to new generations. Of these, only twenty are being spoken, by probably fewer than five hundred people.

To take an example from another sphere: when Roman Catholic schools weaken in the teaching of Latin, and when Protestant clergy are no longer required to learn Hebrew and Greek, the confidence which the rest of us may have in their capacity to preserve the traditions by which they live must be diminished. We cannot share the vision of medieval Catholicism, or for that matter of the Protestant reformation unless there are some around us who can read Latin; and we cannot begin to be confident that the Hebrew Scriptures or the New Testament are being reliably interpreted unless there are some who know the languages in which they were written.

To turn to the so-called multicultural scene, it is difficult to see how we can gain an understanding of cultures other than those into which we were born without at least some of us learning their languages; and perhaps everyone learning some language. The first reason for selecting Italian or Greek or any other contemporary language to be taught in primary and secondary schools is that there are Italians and Greeks in the community who will welcome it; or perhaps that we owe it to those communities to help them to keep the language alive among their children. But there is a second reason, at least every bit as compelling as the first: some of the rest of us should be learning these languages so that we can see the world through another set of spectacles. There will be no shared vision worth having in Australia that is not stereoscopic: to see the world in all its many dimensions we must not be content with single vision.

Perhaps we should be a little careful in our use of the phrase 'community languages'. All languages belong to communities; but it should not count for nothing that some communities have brought forth a Dante or a Boccaccio or a Petrarch, and that the tradition of perceptive writing continues into our own day. As we said in another connection in an earlier chapter, some things are worth doing for their own sake. To learn Greek or Italian or one of a number of other languages is worthwhile not only in order to be able to converse with a neighbour, but also because it is interesting: the world can become a richer place; it is worth exploring. The reward is in the learning, in the reading.

This leads to my next reflection. We in Australia have received into the membership of this people, men and women who in their own persons or the persons of their families have passed through some of the most traumatic experiences of the human race in the twentieth century: war, famine, totalitarian regimes of the right and the left, racial oppression. If we were to confine ourselves to reading the literature written by native-born Australians in the past fifty or sixty years, we would indeed be a thriftless people. I do not mean that we should not read our own writers—of course not. There, too, however, we would sometimes not understand what our own poets and novelists are writing about if we were to limit ourselves to them alone. I can think of poems by A.D. Hope and Vincent Buckley (to go no further) which would be largely incomprehensible if we did not allow for their wider sympathies and sensibilities. But what I want to plead for goes beyond that.

Paul Tillich, the German philosophical theologian the centenary of whose birth was celebrated a year ago, makes use of the distinction between two Greek words for time: *chronos*, from which we get chronology, chronometer, refers to time measured horizontally as it were; *kairos* refers to the appropriate time, a critical time—time measured by the height or depth of its significance, vertically as it were. Human history, Tillich argued, has had *kairoi*, critical moments that disclose to men and women things of significance for the whole of life: moments of truth, as we should say. In the twentieth century, we have known a number of these: life as it was lived, and death as it was died, in Nazi Germany; the fate of the Jews and other dissidents in Stalinist Russia; the liberation of church groups and others in Latin

America; the whole story of Jewish emancipation. For any one of these—or other examples—to have become a moment of truth someone had to write about it or perhaps paint about it, or write music about it. What those moments had to teach us—or as some would put it, what God had to teach us (all of us) through those moments—had to be articulated.

Anna Akhmatova was already a poet in Russia before the revolution. She lived the rest of her life there until she died in 1966. Mercifully much of her story and much of her poetry has survived and been translated into English. She seems to have asked constantly three questions: what does it mean in these terrible days to be a Russian? what does it mean to be a Russian woman? and what does it mean to be a Russian woman who is a poet?

No foreign sky protected me,
no stranger's wing shielded my face.
I stand as witness to the common lot,
survivor of that time, that place

she wrote in 1961. A few years previously she had told this story:

In the terrible years of the Yezhov terror I spent seventeen months waiting in line outside the prison in Leningrad. One day somebody in the crowd identified me. Standing behind me was a woman, with lips blue from the cold, who had, of course, never heard me called by name before. Now she started out of the torpor common to us all and asked me in a whisper (everyone whispered there): 'Can you describe this?' And I said: 'I can.' Then something like a smile passed fleetingly over what had once been her face.

Akhmatova's determination was 'not to forget' and 'not to allow to be forgotten'.

If we lose the freshness of words,
The simplicity of feeling,
Is it not like an artist losing his sight,
An actor—his voice and movement,
A splendid woman, her beauty?

But don't try to keep for yourself
What has been the gift of Heaven:
Our lot as we ourselves know
Is to squander, not to save.

Go alone and heal the blind,
And in the difficult hour of doubt,

See your disciples jeer and gloat
And know the indifference of the crowd.

D.M. Thomas, an English novelist and poet, has written:

> Akhmatova herself, with her great compeers, Mandelstam, Pasternak and Tsvetaeva, must be accounted largely responsible for the continuity of Russian poetic tradition. Together, they made it possible for the people to continue to draw strength from them . . . (Akhmatova outlived the other three, but) all four had overcome. The officials of Stalin's monolith were retiring 'to rest in card indexes' in studies of their work. It is a momentous thought. Can it be by chance that the worst of times found the best of poets to wage the war for eternal truth and human dignity?

One cannot resist asking: which of the figures whose names appear most prominently in our newspapers will in due course 'rest in card indexes', and who will prove to have spoken for eternal truth and human dignity?

I have spent some time on this example not because many of our fellow Australians suffered directly from Stalin's terror although some did; but that is not the point. That *kairos*, that significant point in human affairs, disclosed to us all who live towards the end of the twentieth century facts that we ignore to our peril, or at least to our impoverishment. The chief fact disclosed is not that Stalin was a wicked man. That does not require much demonstration. What has been disclosed is the power of words, or as Akhmatova would have said, resting firmly in the Christian tradition, the power of the Word to speak for human dignity, to hold people in hope in the midst of despair; and with whatever air of sadness or melancholy to speak of the priority of love and friendship in human relations: at whatever cost, to demonstrate that power—sheer brute physical or psychological power—does not have the last word in the affairs of men and women. Here at work, in Vincent Buckley's phrase, is 'the language in which the sacred is not only expressed but approached'.

Let me take another example, for it will illustrate the variety of ways in which other people's stories will help us to understand them more deeply—as well as give us great pleasure in the learning. I refer to the writings of the Jewish author Isaac Bashevis Singer, born in Poland in 1904, his father and his grandfather both Rabbis, he himself educated in the Warsaw Rabbinical Seminary. He left Poland in 1935, and has since then lived in the United States of America. His writings are in Yiddish, but many have been translated into English, most of them by members of his family or close friends. In 1978 he was awarded the Nobel Prize for Literature. For present purposes he is of interest to us for three reasons.

First are his accounts of Jewish families, almost as sagas. His two-volume novel *The Manor* and *The Estate* tells the story of Jacoby Calman and his family from the time of the Polish insurrection against the Tsar in 1863 until the end of the century. He had previously written *The Family Moskat*, which covers the period from the turn of the century until the German invasion of 1939. On any showing it is a period and a place of great interest for understanding the modern world; but for us in Australia these novels are important because they portray the problems of an older people with older ways coming to terms with modern industrial civilization, with Western modernity, if you like to put it that way. It is the story of the emergence of the Polish Jews from their ghetto into an industrial society, of how some looked West and went to America or Palestine—of the Zionist dream and the quest for security—of how others came to terms with German philosophy or revolutionary politics, of the effect of the break up of the old family morality. Through it all it is the story of people on the move, into a society that was new and strange to them, and of the tests to which traditional beliefs and relationships are put.

The second element in Singer's writings to which I would draw attention is his short stories. They deal with many different themes, with old age and childhood; they have many central characters from a chimney sweep to a rich widow; their setting may be Warsaw, New York, or Tel Aviv, the passengers in a crowded bus may 'curse each other in Yiddish, Polish, German or broken Hebrew', but all the tales are held within the one vision. The stories are not forced into an ideological mould, or used for propaganda, but they have a certain philosophical coherence, a calm acceptance of and a loving detachment from the tradition to which the author belongs. One may contrast some contemporary Australian short stories that sometimes isolate an incident or mood without providing a framework (albeit quiescently or latently) within which these aspects of life may be understood; at others the ideological presupposition is all too apparent.

This leads to a third aspect of Singer's work: the re-telling of older Jewish narratives, the imaginative reconstruction of tales about magical persons or holy men or women in the past. The fanciful note is never far from being struck; and a new world, peopled however strangely, fills our mind. We learn about a people and their culture having psychic or imaginative depth in a way that would otherwise be denied to us. Andrew Fletcher of Saltoun in the seventeenth century 'knew a very wise man who believed if a man were permitted to make all the ballads, he need not care who should make the laws of a nation'. We might extend that and say that if we know a people's imaginative literature we may be less concerned with their constitutional history: if we knew the stories of the Dreamtime, and gave ourselves opportunities to stand reflectively before Aboriginal art, we might have fewer problems in coming to terms with political accommodation. We could go on multiplying examples: one of the advances in New Testament studies in the twentieth century has brought about an increasing awareness that the parables of Jesus are not moral tales told for the improvement of our behaviour, they are translucent moments at which a light breaks through and shows the world in different colours—rather like the sunlight shining through stained glass. What Jesus called the Kingdom of God breaks in through these stories. They are not primarily stories about dogma or ethics. They are illuminations, from which right teaching and good conduct may flow.

Think of the friend who comes at midnight: he is embarrassed, a friend of his has come and needs sustenance, three loaves. Will you lie in bed and deny him this? It is unlikely. You may be inclined to lie in bed and ignore the normal conventions of hospitality. Nevertheless something of the shamelessness of the circumstances rouses you. His need and your character meet, so you get up and do something about it. What does that tell you about the relation between God and men?

I have concentrated on two places where the human voice of our time may be heard in such a way as to quicken imagination, arouse sympathy and prepare us to hear it elsewhere. This is only a beginning. The great stories of the human race must be told and heard again and again: the story of Odysseus and of his journey and homecoming; the story of the Iliad, and of the tragic conflicts of war. Fundamental to our understanding of Western, and for that matter Eastern and Middle Eastern, culture is the story of Moses, with all its many layers and implications. This is a story that has given us the word and the notion of emancipation: the liberation of slaves from captivity in Egypt. 'Let my people go.' That story has provided us with the figure who after that of Jesus Christ has haunted Western and Eastern Orthodox art more than any other.

Speaking of Moses' birth and upbringing, a nineteeth-century Christian preacher could say: 'That child who might have become so degraded, stands second but to One in dignity and influence in the annals of the human race.'

Yet, do these stories belong to the education of young Australians? I doubt it. We seem more anxious to put before them what is believed to be accessible, within their present experience, which is necessarily small and limited. We do well to remember, however, that children of all ages (and that includes you and me) are sometimes likely to be moved and permanently affected by what is outside our reach, but which comes to us through the imagination by metaphor and symbol and story. This frequently turns out to be inherently interesting. Perhaps if we were to start with what the human race has found fascinating we would begin to see what in the great volume of talented writing available from the pens of Australians of many different backgrounds is most worthy of attention.

We began this chapter with a quotation from George Eliot who saw so much of what goes to make up human life, its relations, its responsibilities, its foibles, by looking intensively into the society of one part of England, not indeed in her own day, but immediately after the passing of the Reform Bill of 1832. 'A book of more breadth of genius in conception, of more even execution is hardly to be found in our language,' said one contemporary of *Middlemarch*. Yet a present-day critic can be 'tempted [I use his words] into scolding her for not doing what no English novelist of the century did: for not taking possession of the great world'. Tolstoy and Dostoyevsky and Flaubert do that: they see in the story they have to tell something of the fate of the human race.

In Australia we have a growing and notable literature that looks intensively at our past and at some of the joys and foibles of the present. There are some writers and artists and painters who have also begun to take possession of the great world. They are a formidable array, and we need them all, if the domestic context and the fate of the human race are to be held together in our imagination. Without an ever enriched and transformed imagination we are unlikely to acquire a shared vision.

5

Some Larger Love or Loyalty

In a previous chapter I spoke about some of the ways in which our patterns of behaviour are controlled by conventions. I introduced this by references to the behaviour of members of professions. But conventions influence other relations of life. Gilbert Harman writes:

> Moralities are social. They are defined by the conventions of groups. But you belong to more than one group, and different groups have different conventions. Which conventions determine your moral obligations? They all do. Since you belong to a number of different groups, you are subject to a number of different moralities—the morality of your family, perhaps your school, a professional morality (your 'business ethics'), the morality of your neighborhood, the various moralities of various groups of friends, the morality of your country, and finally, perhaps, a limited morality you share with most of humanity. These moralities will sometimes be in conflict, and give rise to a tragic situation in which you are faced with a conflict of loyalties. In that case, there is no clear moral solution to your problem. You must choose the group which is most important to you and act on its conventions.

I do not suppose that Professor Harman would offer that as an exhaustive list. We in Australia would certainly want to draw attention to the conventions that determine moral obligations as we have inherited them in different ethnic groups: our cultural conventions, our conventional moralities deriving from different religious positions, or political convictions. The question that we have set ourselves is this: are there any perceptions that we have in common that transcend these differences? There are some, we said; or there should be some. A healthy, and to some extent cohesive, society depends upon a reasonable proportion of its citizens having a common respect for certain things (what we called an awareness of the sacred); it equally depends on groups of people working out the ethical implications of being members of a particular profession, or of pursuing a particular occupation; and all the time we need to be having our outlook enriched and transformed by the quickening of our imaginations.

Is there anything more to be said about our shared vision, matters that we could look at through common eyes in such a way as ultimately to determine public policy? I have no doubt that there are several, but I want to select three: a common awareness of the importance of the family as the basic unit of society; a common determination that every member of the community should be provided with an opportunity to work; and a commitment to improve the quality of life for all citizens but especially for those whose lives have been rendered poor or mean.

The many cultures to which we in Australia belong bring with them a great variety of patterns of family life, from the tribal loyalties of Aborigines to the small unit of the nuclear family with its 2.4 children. Few institutions in our society have been subjected to closer analysis. The family has been dissected and defended from as many points of view as there are articulate social scientists or imaginative writers. We are all experts on families, for we have all been—all are—members of families, whether they are happy and contented or places of tension and disruption.

After all the battering that the family has received from supporters and critics, two things seem to have emerged, which must belong to our shared vision. The first is that the family, nuclear and where possible extended, continues to be the primary unit in which we care for one another, not only at the beginning of life (infancy and childhood) or at the end of life (old age, declining powers, decrepitude), but also in the middle of life when apparently we are strong. The second is that the family is the primary place of experience of moral realities: the place where we learn to talk, and to speak the truth, to love and be loved.

Because the family is the primary unit of care, its protection has almost always been the subject of legislation. For long that seemed to be confined to laws relating to marriage, but when social legislation gained in prominence and the state took responsibility to support families, at least families in need, the focus shifted from concern with marriage to concern with the protection of women and children. The state today has to recognize a greater variety of patterns of family life than in the past—for instance, with the growing incidence of one-parent families—but a responsibility towards the family in some shape or form is one from which no government can be allowed to walk away.

At the other end, from matters on which we depend on legislation, the family is shaped by conventions that we observe. These conventions include family Christmas parties or the observance of Mother's Day or of birthdays. For centuries Jews have known the value of the observance of Sabbath Eve in the home. There are, however, other kinds of conventions that need to be observed. It is difficult to state them without sounding banal or naive, but a fundamental convention is a respect for truth. By this I do not mean that members of a family should always, painfully, be telling each other what they think. I mean rather what some Hebrew and Greek writers meant when they equated truth with reliability. Members of a family should be able to depend upon one another.

This is most vividly expressed in the commitment made by a man and a woman each to the other in marriage. Today there may be more de facto relationships than heretofore: many would claim that they have as deep a commitment to each other as married couples. Nevertheless, most children are born within a formalized marriage relationship, and there is much to be learnt from that relationship. Both by common law and by the law of the church, men and women married each other in the exchange of vows. A vow is something different from an aspiration or a good intention. An exchange of vows is something more than a legal contract (though it may involve that), more than a socially convenient way of announcing to friends and relatives that a couple now intend to live together (if they have indeed not already been doing so), more than a dramatic way of expressing a romantic attachment; it is a determination to live together for better for worse, for richer for poorer, and so on—till death do us part. Life is no longer to be lived by inclination but to be controlled by commitment.

We can say that and still be sympathetic when things go wrong. Few experiences are more painful than disruptions within a family. But the point is that we can and should use the phrase 'things go wrong'. W.H. Auden wrote a poem entitled *Their Lonely*

Betters. He describes how he 'listened . . . in the shade/To all the noises that my garden made'—the robins singing and the flowers rustling.

No one of them was capable of lying,
There was not one which knew that it was dying . . .
Let them leave language to their lonely betters
Who count some days and long for certain letters;
We, too, make noises when we laugh or weep:
Words are for those with promises to keep.

It is in the family that we learn to speak, it is there that we should learn to speak the truth, it is there that we have to learn to abide by promises. It is in the family that we learn that there are other people in the world who are more important than we are; and that moving out in concentric circles we should enter into relationships of confidence and trust, in which constancy and loyalty are regarded as virtues.

After the family I suppose that one of the next areas in which most men and women find themselves in contact with other people is the workplace; and I have suggested as part of our shared vision a common determination that every member of our community should be provided with an opportunity to work. There are some resemblances and some differences between life in the family and life at work; and they may both—the resemblances and the differences—be instructive.

First we might note in passing that, as with the family, we all tend to have opinions about work: we have worked, or we hope to work, or we have been denied work, or we have had work to do that was satisfying or not satisfying. Some have had experience of working with their hands, some predominantly working with their brains, some know a lot about working at a desk—on paper or with a computer—some spend most of their time working with people, seeing them face to face, co-operating with others obtaining their co-operation, in competition with others, outwitting them perhaps. And the relation between effort and financial reward varies enormously. Some know what they will earn this week, this month, this and next year; and the sum is not going to vary according to the amount of effort put into their work. Others find their income affected directly by the number of hours given to their work, and the quality of their performance. Some again find that their earnings depend on factors largely beyond their own control, the weather, the price of basic commodities in overseas markets, or what the public (which is fickle in this regard) is prepared to pay for works of art or regards as entertainment.

These distinctions do not exhaust accounts of the different ways in which we experience work, or the different points at which we are denied it; but they suggest that when we talk about the importance of providing men and women with opportunities to work we are talking about a lot of different situations in life. Just as the family provides men and women and children with the primary unit in which they are cared for (or at least that is as it should be), so work and the workplace provide or should provide men and women with the security of having a purposeful existence. Different cultures will give different reasons for this phenomenon. That is to say, there will be a variety of explanations at the ultimate level, arising from fundamental convictions about man's nature. For our purpose we may observe that we deny men and women something that belongs to their human nature when we deprive them of the opportunity to work. Work can be part of their joy in sharing in creative activity, whether it expresses the human race's relation to nature, industrial development, commercial expansion, economic growth, or social organization: in all these ways, men and women fulfil a part of their nature through work. One strand in our cultural tradition—that which goes back to the Hebrews—while stressing that work should be enjoyable notes also that work is an economic necessity, and that it sometimes involves drudgery. These are important reminders that the criterion by which we judge work is not simply whether it is invariably enjoyable; we judge it rather by whether it is genuinely creative and productive. In passing we might note that it is always safer to apply this reminder about the drudgery that is part of work to ourselves than it is to apply it to others. It would be a distortion in our understanding of what work does for a man or woman—giving them a joyful part in creative activity—to chain some to a ceaseless drudgery.

Again just as surely as the family is the place where we first meet the moral reality of other people with whom we must live, so the workplace in its way is also an arena where moral considerations enter into our relations one with another. The way in which we describe the moral considerations that enter in differs in the two cases. The family operates on ethical considerations expressed in terms of love and trust and forgiveness. The workplace operates with a more impersonal morality of loyalty, reliability and above all fairness or justice. Archbishop William Temple once described justice as love operating at a distance. I cannot express my concern for my fellow human being in Africa through the exercise of personal virtues which I must practise inside my family. If I really care for him or her, if I really want to love those distant neighbours as myself, I will seek justice for them—a fair deal, access to the courts to right their wrongs, an impartial hearing of cases, a just reward for labour. Such matters may require political and legislative action: only thus can justice be done, or attempted, and love become effective at a distance.

Similarly with the provision of work for every man or woman who wishes to take advantage of it. There is an abiding imperative, to provide work for others because to deny it is to destroy part of what it is to be human—just as surely as the destruction of a man's language reduces his humanity. Not any work on any conditions, but work that is rewarded on a scale consistent with a man or woman's dignity as a citizen of this country in the closing decades of the twentieth century. If that is too general and vague, then let us discover what it means; but we have set the problem for economists and politicians and social workers and theorists to solve. We do not accept as inevitable that a considerable residue of man and woman power in this country is condemned to be without purposeful work.

If Hugh Stretton is right in saying that a return to full or fuller employment can not be achieved by the traditional macroeconomic means alone, then, in his words:

> We need also some old and some new micro-economic policies. They might include more education, training and retraining; more work-sharing by a range of means from part-timing through shorter working hours to wider uses of sabbatical long-service and retraining leave; some increase of taxation and collective spending on public goods and services; some public or subsidized-private 'employer of last resort'.

It is no part of the purpose of these lectures to discuss the economic or political actions necessary for the restoration to the vast majority of citizens of this country the opportunity to work, to work productively and to be given a fair reward. It is appropriate to say that these must be part of the shared vision of our society, and that we look to those in authority to tell us not what will not work but of those things to which we may put our hand that may be effective.

Let me repeat: the demand for work for all is rooted in a conviction that a man or woman's humanity is to a high degree bound up with his or her having meaningful work to do. And the provision of work must be within terms that are just and seen to be just. Augustine said:

> Set justice aside and what are kingdoms but large robber bands, and what are robber bands but little kingdoms . . . Excellent and elegant was the pirate's answer to the great Macedonian Alexander, who had taken him. The king asking him how he durst molest the seas so, he replied with a free spirit, 'How darest thou molest the whole world? But because I do it with a little ship only I am called a thief, thou doing it with a great navy art called a conqueror.'

Justice demands a certain degree of equity, of fairness.

This leads to the third of our considerations: a shared vision will include a commitment to improve the quality of life for all citizens. In the second chapter I spoke of some of the things that point beyond ourselves, indicators of the sacred. I suppose it might have been entitled 'Man does not live by bread alone'. Throughout I have tried to say that there are considerations that make life worth living that go beyond what can be required by law, that there are people and values that triumph over brute force, and that our own concern that our fellowman or woman should have meaningful work is rooted not simply in the economic self-interest of the community—namely, that we cannot afford to have so much labour power idle, although that is true—it is rooted rather in what is their due as human beings. We now note that part of our shared vision is of a community that cares for the quality of life of its members.

In 1940, when Britain was desperately fighting for survival, the historian E.H. Carr (himself certainly a realist) wrote in an editorial for *The Times*:

> If we speak of democracy, we do not mean a democracy which maintains the right to vote and forgets the right to work and the right to live. If we speak of freedom, we do not mean a rugged individualism which excluded social organization and economic planning. If we speak of equality, we do not mean a political equality nullified by social and economic privilege. If we speak of economic reconstructions, we think less of maximum production, though this too will be required, than of equitable distribution.

A year later William Temple, then Archbishop of Canterbury, first used the term, 'welfare state': this in contrast to what Carr had called the 'night watchman state' of the nineteenth century. The state was there, it was argued, not simply to guard you against night marauders but to promote the health, education and welfare of all its members.

The notion of the welfare state is now less popular than it was. Indeed, some in public life compete if not in denigrating it then in distancing themselves from the term and the reality that it represents. Nevertheless, it is worth taking it out and examining it again. Is it true, for instance, that we cannot afford to have a universal welfare system? We are told that it is too costly and that taxes must come down not go up. But it has been pointed out that the tax revolt of recent years did not occur in the countries with the highest level of taxation (Scandinavia and the Germanic countries) but in Anglo-Saxon countries with relatively low levels of tax by OECD standards. It may be significant that the higher taxed countries also had a universal welfare system from which both rich and poor benefited. Everybody could see how their taxes might help them. In countries like ours, where it is thought that benefits should be directed to the needs of the poor alone, there is a demand for tax cuts: the rich and the middle class feel that they are being asked to provide for the poor, and there are even some who say that they are being asked to provide for the improvident. The situation might be quite different if we were more actively concerned about the quality of life of the whole community.

Another example: never before in the history of Australia have works of art been purchased for such inflated prices as has happened in the art auctions of recent months and years. Private individuals are spending a lot of money on what we might term aggrandisement. Yet we have museums and galleries and libraries quite inadequately supported by private or public funds. We're back at the bad old contrast: private affluence, public, if not squalor, then need. There is a terrible nemesis ahead for a country that allows expenditure on higher education to decline over a twelve-year period from 1.73 per cent to 0.9 per cent of gross domestic product.

I cite these instances not in order to offer solutions but to raise questions for debate and to ask how serious we are about the improvement of the quality of life for all citizens. Such a quality of life, of course, has to be paid for. In the process, some of the rich will be a little less rich and some of the poor a little less poor. It is by no means clear, however, that this country would be less secure financially and economically if we were to pay as much attention to the quality of life as to the quantity of goods which we possess or process. Nor is it by any means clear, despite some current orthodoxies, that public expenditure is rarely as beneficial as private expenditure or that public borrowing is more improvident than private borrowing. There would seem to be a case for looking at instances on their merits.

Because the examples given are worrying, I could leave a negative, not to say depressing impression. If we look at the three areas about which I have been speaking in this chapter—family, work, quality of life—there is much to hearten us. Many of the cultures now present in this country have brought with them a strong family life and loyalty: where they are available, within reach, members support each other to an impressive degree. Many of the educational initiatives, some of them taken quite locally, say in TAFE colleges, have prepared young people for specific occupations in the areas in which they live, and have re-trained older people (not least middle-aged women) to enable them to undertake satisfying, useful and productive work. No one can travel through the country districts of Victoria, or (I imagine) of other states, without coming across heartening instances of local government, in the words of one municipal officer, discovering afresh that their responsibility is not only to the preservation and enhancement of property, but also to serve people: quality of life is on the agenda, but it is also on the ground, with initiatives being taken by local business sometimes quite small but contributing to employment, to the enrichment of life *and* to the country's export earnings; also quality of life, in the growth and development of crafts, in the provision of sporting facilities and the encouragement of physical fitness.

So we could multiply examples of what is heartening. This needs to be said to offset the widespread preoccupation with self and self-fulfilment: too many marriages break up because *I*, the first person singular, am not satisfied or fulfilled, or because *I* the first person singular, have become tired of making a daily effort to live with and to love this partner or take daily responsibility for these children. We are surrounded by public exhortations to gain satisfaction by a therapy that will look after *me*, the first person singular now in the accusative case, to make purchases, even to borrow from the banks to do so in such a way as to make *me* ride higher, look more beautiful or successful among my contemporaries. There is nothing wrong with beauty or success, but plenty that is questionable about the way in which it is to be achieved. What Hugh Stretton has called the cult of selfishness has to be resisted. Self-respect is one thing; self-obsession is another.

If we are to withstand the massive selfcentredness that characterizes personal and organized or institutional life at the end of the twentieth century, many people will have to live in ways that cost them something: the only way to overcome selfishness is by unselfishness. Is there, in a phrase of Reinhold Niebuhr, 'some larger love or loyalty which qualifies the self-interest of various groups'—something that we have or could have in common, at what I have called the penultimate level? I think there is.

Many men and women came to this country, many men and women have grown up in this country, with a hope in their hearts that they and their children might see and know a fairer, more just and compassionate society than has been known in previous generations in this country or in the countries they came from. We should be careful not to allow that hope to grow dim. Many men and women have believed that there is an order of truth and beauty and goodness that transcends their immediate desires and judges their earthbound self-regarding natures. We should be careful not to denigrate the intellectual curiosity, sensitive imagination, or religious conviction on which such a belief depends. Many men and women have perceived—in another phrase of Niebuhr—that 'nothing we do, however virtuous, can be accomplished alone; therefore we must be saved by love'. We should be careful not to quench that fire: it is altogether too easy to stop loving your fellow man or woman, and to stop them loving each other.

Hope, faith, love: they are the conditions of civilized life in a secular society just as surely as they have their roots for some in a religious context. And did not somebody say that the greatest of these is love?—the eye that is constantly looking out on the world in all its wonder, and on the neighbour in his or her need.

Notes

The notion of a shared vision is prominent in the writings on multiculturalism of Professor Jerzy Zubrzycki. Most recently he has written:

> The future vision of a multicultural Australia must be a shared one because only then can cultural diversity and national cohesion co-exist within the one economic and political unit. Such a vision implies a powerful commitment to two principles: first, that equality is there for people to be different; and, second that the motive force of society should be moral improvement.
> 'Public Policy in a Multicultural Australia', *Quadrant*, July 1987, pp. 48–52.

In these lectures I have tried to accept the challenge implied in those words, and can only encourage readers to pursue the topic further through Professor Zubrzycki's writings.

I

Who Are We?

In the preparation of the first lecture, I found help in J. M. Cuddihy, *The Ordeal of Civility* (Basic Books, New York, 1974), in Maurice Cranston's article 'Toleration' in *The Encyclopedia of Philosophy*, ed. Paul Edwards (Macmillan, New York, 1967), and that on 'Religious Toleration' by Elisabeth Labrousse in the *Dictionary of the History of Ideas*, ed. Philip P. Wiener (Scribner, New York, 1973). The literature on Roman Catholic and Jewish emancipation is immense. I gained illumination from Jacob Katz, 'The Term "Jewish Emancipation": its Origin and Historical Impact' in *Studies in Nineteenth-Century Jewish Intellectual History*, ed. Alex. Altmann (Cambridge, Harvard University Press, 1964).

John Locke's *Epistola de Tolerantia* is conveniently translated by J.W. Gough with an introduction by Raymond Klibansky (Oxford, 1968).

Patrick O'Farrell's *The Irish in Australia* was published by the University of New South Wales Press in 1986.

2

Something Beyond Ourselves

The passage from Solzhenitsyn is taken from a piece entitled 'Along the Oka' to be found in *Patriarchs and Prophets: Persecution of the Russian Orthodox Church*, ed. Michael Bourdeaux (Mowbrays, London, 1975). The notion of the penultimate is taken from Dietrich Bonhoeffer, *Ethics* (SCM Press, London, 1955). The lines from Judith Wright are quoted from a poem entitled 'Nigger's Leap, New England' to be found in *The New Oxford Book of Australian Verse*, ed. Les A. Murray (OUP, Melbourne, 1986) and in her *Collected Poems* 1942–70 (Angus & Robertson, Sydney, 1975). Much that is said about science was learnt from Michael Polanyi and in particular from his Gifford Lectures *Personal Knowledge: Towards a Post-Critical Philosophy* (Routledge & Kegan Paul, London, 1962).

3

Professions and Conventions

On 'conventions' and 'professional ethics' see the articles under these headings, and bibliography provided, by G. R. Dunstan and Dorothy Emmet in *A New Dictionary of Christian Ethics*, ed. John Macquarrie and James Childress (SCM Press, London, 1986). Also the article 'Declarations' in *Dictionary of Medical Ethics*, ed. A. S. Duncan, G. R. Dunstan, R. B. Welbourn (London, 1981). See too G. R. Dunstan, *The Artifice of Ethics* (London, 1978); Dorothy Emmet, *Rules, Roles and Relations* (London, 1967), *Function, Purpose & Powers* (Temple University Press, 1972); Gilbert Harman *The Nature of Morality* (Oxford University Press, New York, 1977). John Nieuwenhuysen and Marina Williams-Wynn's *Professions in the Marketplace* was published by Melbourne University Press in 1982. Richard M. Titmuss used the phrase 'the gift relationship' in his study *The Gift Relationship* (Allen & Unwin, London, 1970), see too his *Commitment to Welfare* (London, 1973).

4

Ourselves Writ Strange

John Dunmore Lang's 'Colonial Nomenclature' is to be found in *The New Oxford Book of Australian Verse*, ed. Les A. Murray (OUP, Melbourne, 1986). On Anna Akhmatova see Amanda Haight, *Akhmatova: a Poetic Pilgrimage* (OUP, London, 1976); *Poems of Akhmatova*, selected, translated and introduced by Stanley Kunitz with Max Hayward (Collins & Harvill, London, 1974), and *You Will Hear Thunder*, Poems translated by D. M. Thomas (Secker & Warburg, London, 1985). The novels and many of the short stories of Isaac Bashevis Singer are published by Penguin Books and by Farrar, Straus and Giroux, New York.

5

Some Larger Love or Loyalty

The poem by W. H. Auden 'Their Lonely Betters' may be found in *Collected Shorter Poems 1927–57* (Faber, London, 1966). The quotation from Hugh Stretton is taken from his *Political Essays* (Georgian House, Melbourne, 1987), a book demonstrating an unusual blend of social and economic analysis and moral indignation, which if taken seriously could have a salutary effect on public attitudes. The reference to E. H. Carr's editorial in *The Times* I owe to Asa Briggs, *A Social History of England* (Weidenfeld and Nicholson, London, 1983). Had space permitted I would like to have referred to Stuart Macintyre, *Winners and Losers: the pursuit of social justice in Australian history* (Allen & Unwin, Sydney, 1985), a reminder of how difficult it is to realize the vision of a more just society. Archbishop Temple's use of the term 'welfare state' appears in *Citizen and Churchman*: see Ronald Preston's article, 'Welfare State' in *A New Dictionary of Christian Ethics*. The quotations from Reinhold Niebuhr are taken from *Christian Realism and Political Problems* (Faber, London, 1954) and *The Irony of American History* (Scribner, New York, 1962).

Acknowledgements

The author and publisher wish to thank the following authors and publishers for permission to reprint their material.

The extract from the poem, Niggers Leap, New England, by Judith Wright from her book Collected Poems 1942–1970 (© Judith Wright, 1971, Angus & Robertson) is reproduced with permission. The extract from *Anna Akhmatova: A Poetic Pilgrimage* by Amanda Haight (Oxford University Press) is reproduced with permission. The extract from *You Will Hear Thunder* by D.M. Thomas (Secker and Warbug) is reproduced with permission.